BUILDING BLOCKS OF GEOGRAPHY

PLACES AND REGIONS

Written by Izzi Howell

Illustrated by Steve Evans

WORLD BOOK

a Scott Fetzer company
Chicago

World Book, Inc.
180 North LaSalle Street
Suite 900
Chicago, Illinois 60601
USA

For information about other World Book publications,
visit our website at **www.worldbook.com**
or call **1-800-WORLDBK (967-5325)**.
For information about sales to schools and libraries,
call 1-800-975-3250 (United States),
or 1-800-837-5365 (Canada).

Library of Congress Cataloging-in-Publication Data
for this volume has been applied for.

Building Blocks of Geography
ISBN: 978-0-7166-4275-6 (set, hc.)

Places and Regions
ISBN: 978-0-7166-4285-5 (hc.)

Also available as:
ISBN: 978-0-7166-4295-4 (e-book)

1st printing June 2022

WORLD BOOK STAFF
Executive Committee
President: Geoff Broderick
Vice President, Editorial: Tom Evans
Vice President, Finance: Donald D. Keller
Vice President, Marketing: Jean Lin
Vice President, International: Eddy Kisman
Vice President, Technology: Jason Dole
Director, Human Resources: Bev Ecker

Editorial
Manager, New Content: Jeff De La Rosa
Associate Manager, New Product:
    Nicholas Kilzer
Sr. Editor: Shawn Brennan
Proofreader: Nathalie Strassheim

Graphics and Design
Sr. Visual Communications Designer:
    Melanie Bender
Sr. Web Designer/Digital Media Developer:
    Matt Carrington
Coordinator, Design Development:
    Brenda Tropinski

Acknowledgments:
Writer: Izzi Howell
Illustrator: Steve Evans
Series advisor: Marjorie Frank

Developed with World Book by
White-Thomson Publishing LTD

www.wtpub.co.uk

TABLE OF CONTENTS

There is a glossary on page 40. Terms defined in the glossary are in type **that looks like this** on their first appearance.

What do the Taj Mahal ...

... the Sahara Desert ...

... Australia ...

... and Grand Central Station in New York City have in common?

They're all places, just like me! Geography is all about different places around the world. We give names to special or important places.

A place can be naturally occurring, such as the Nile River ...

... or human-made, like the city of Abu Dhabi in the United Arab Emirates.

It could be one specific building, such as the Leaning Tower of Pisa in Italy ...

... or cover a huge area, like the wild Amazon rain forest in South America.

We can group places together into categories, such as historical sites, **monuments**, countries, **mountain ranges**, islands ... the list goes on and on!

EARTH'S CONTINENTS AND COUNTRIES

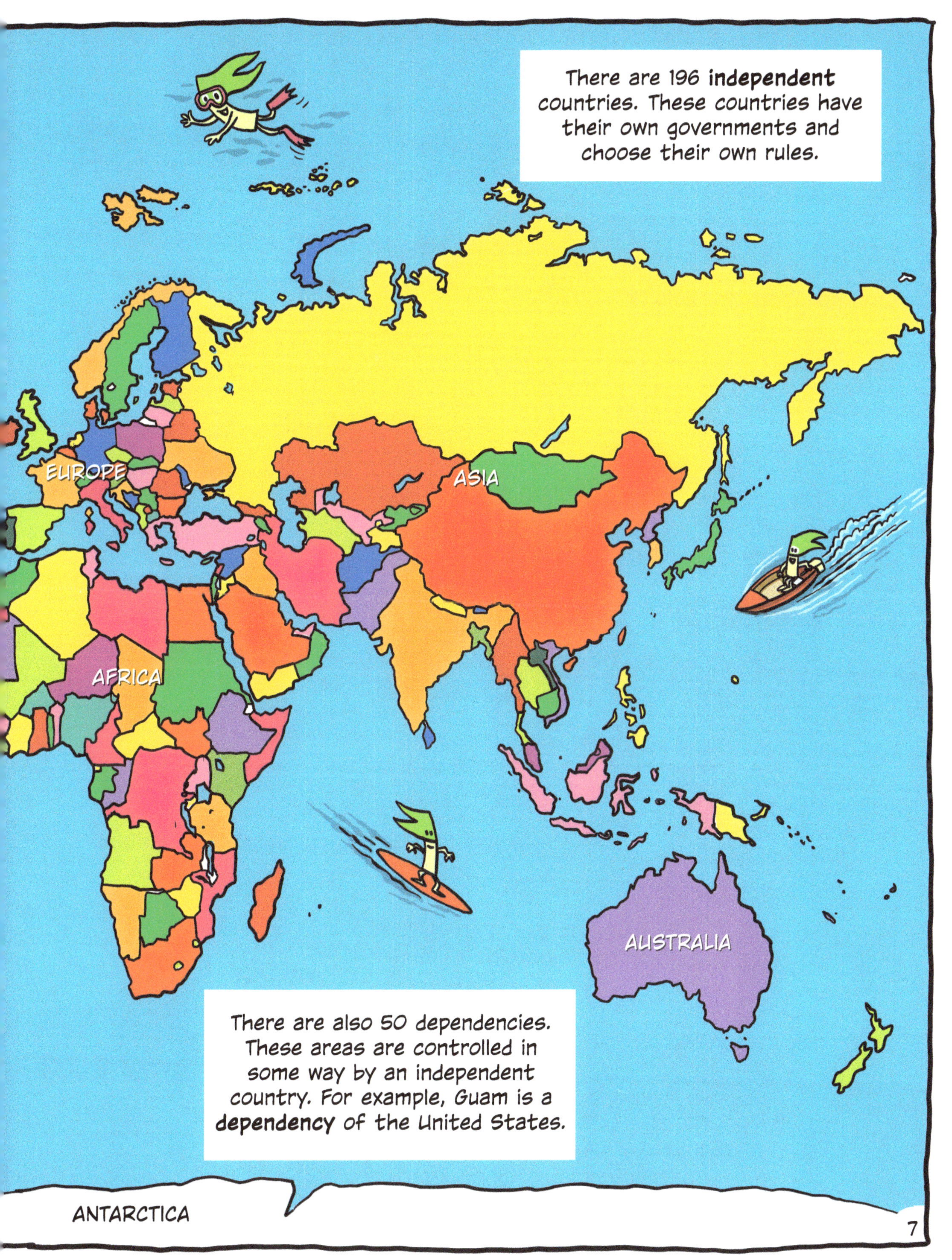

There are 196 **independent** countries. These countries have their own governments and choose their own rules.

There are also 50 dependencies. These areas are controlled in some way by an independent country. For example, Guam is a **dependency** of the United States.

EUROPE
ASIA
AFRICA
AUSTRALIA
ANTARCTICA

If the world handed out prizes, Asia would need a massive shelf for all its trophies! It's a prize-winning place, filled with many other fascinating spots.

Asia is the largest continent in both size and **population**. It is divided up into 50 countries.

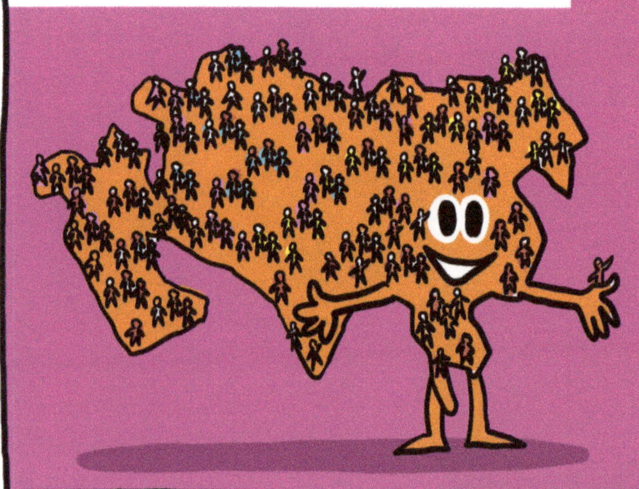

The Asian country of China has the largest population on Earth.

1.4 billion people live in China. That's about 20 percent of the world's population!

Asia is also home to the largest country on Earth—Russia.

Some of the land in Russia also lies in Europe ... shhh!

Some of the largest cities on Earth are found in Asia, such as Tokyo, the capital of Japan.

Not far from Tokyo, you can catch a glimpse of Mount Fuji, the highest mountain in Japan!

Nature can also get pretty big in Asia! Its coastline is the longest of any continent. At about 80,205 miles (129,077 kilometers), this coastline could wrap around the equator three times!
EQUATOR

I'm at the highest point on land, 5 ½ miles (8.85 kilometers) above sea level, at the peak of Mount Everest! The mountain sits on the border between Tibet (China) and Nepal.

Oh, hey Fresh Water! What are you doing here in Russia?
Just checking out my largest lake by volume—Lake Baikal! It contains about one-fifth of the fresh water on Earth's surface.

Wild Bactrian camels live in the Gobi, a desert that stretches across Mongolia and northern China.

If you're interested in amazing buildings in Asia, I know a place or two …
Let's start with historical places!
This is the Great Wall of China. Ancient Chinese rulers built the wall to protect their country from invasion. It's the longest structure ever built!
Go away!

The stunning temple at Angkor Wat, Cambodia, dates from the 1100's. It's the world's largest religious structure.

The beautiful Taj Mahal in India is actually the tomb of an Indian ruler and his wife. Built in the 1600's, it took 20,000 workers 20 years to complete!

I feel ever so royal at the Grand Palace in Thailand. It's no wonder— it's been the official home of the Thai royal family since 1782!

There are some incredible modern structures in Asia as well.
The Heydar Aliyev Center in Baku, Azerbaijan, looks more like a sculpture than a building!

This is the Burj Khalifa in Dubai, United Arab Emirates—the tallest building in the world at 2,716 feet (828 meters) tall.
I can barely see the top!

An enormous steel sphere acts as a pendulum inside the Taipei 101 building in Taiwan, helping to stabilize it in the event of an earthquake.

It may look like an alien planet, but I promise you we're still on Earth! At Gardens by the Bay in Singapore, to be precise!
This nature park is filled with **futuristic** vertical gardens and walkways.

The Danyang-Kunshan Grand Bridge in China is the longest bridge in the world, measuring 102 miles (165 kilometers)! Time to sit back and relax!

EUROPE
They say good things come in small packages, and Europe is no exception!
Europe is one of the smallest continents by size, but it's packed full of amazing places across its 49 countries and 5 dependencies.
EUROPE
EUROPE
Europe is home to the smallest country in the world–the Vatican City. It's about the size of an average city park!
VATICAN CITY
ROME ITALY
The entire country is located within the city of Rome, Italy.
After Russia, which is partially in Asia, Ukraine is the largest European country by size. The soil in Ukraine is very **fertile**, which makes it a leading farming region.
12

Europe's high population and small size mean that it's quite densely populated. One of its countries, Monaco, is actually the world's most densely populated country, with over 26,000 inhabitants per square kilometer!

More than two-fifths of the land in the Netherlands used to be covered by the sea, lakes, or wetlands. The Dutch (natives of the Netherlands) used pumps to drain the land and built dike walls to hold the water in place.

Many cities in Europe are world famous. Tourists come from all over to visit their monuments, historical buildings, and cultural places. This is the magnificent Eiffel Tower in Paris, France.

If you're in London, UK, you've got to see Big Ben ...
... Buckingham Palace ...
... and Tower Bridge!

You can't visit Barcelona, Spain, without stopping by the Sagrada Familia cathedral or Parc Güell. The famous Spanish architect Antoni Gaudí designed both places.

Rome, Italy, is filled with ancient buildings built by the Romans. Gladiators fought each other here in the Colosseum.

Plitvice Lakes National Park in Croatia is just one of many incredible natural places in Europe!

Mont Blanc is the highest mountain in the Alps mountain range. It's located on the border between France, Switzerland, and Italy and is very popular with climbers and hikers.

The Greek island of Santorini was formed when a massive volcano erupted thousands of years ago. The eruption was one of the largest in recorded history.

These long, narrow sea inlets found along the coast of Norway are known as fiords.

According to legend, these amazing natural rock columns at the Giant's Causeway in Northern Ireland were built to allow giants to cross the water between Ireland and Scotland!
Today, scientists believe that the columns were actually created by an ancient volcanic eruption.

Africa is the second largest continent by size and population. It is home to over 1.4 billion people and is split into 54 countries and 5 dependencies.

The largest African country by size is Algeria. The Sahara Desert covers 80 percent of the land in Algeria!

The Gambia is the smallest country within **mainland** Africa. It is a narrow strip of land on either side of the Gambia River, measuring just 15 to 30 miles (24 to 48 kilometers) wide.

Nigeria has the largest population of any African country, with over 200 million people. Around half its population lives in **rural** areas ...

... while the other half lives in big cities, such as Lagos. Lagos is actually the most **populous** city in Africa. It's a major financial center with many businesses.

You're spoiled for choice when it comes to natural wonders in Africa! The striking, flat-topped Table Mountain overlooks the city of Cape Town in the country of South Africa.

The Serengeti National Park in Tanzania is the perfect place to spot such wildlife as lions, African elephants, and cheetahs.

Mount Kilimanjaro is the highest mountain in Africa! It's on the border between Tanzania and Kenya.

And of course, Africa has the Nile River, the longest river in the world! It flows for 4,160 miles (6,695 kilometers) through northeast Africa.

Africa is home to many incredible places. Olduvai Gorge in Tanzania is one of the spots where humanity itself began! Here, scientists have found fossilized **prehistoric** human bones that are nearly 2 million years old.

I'm talking about the ancient Egyptian civilization, of course! You can still see the remains of many ancient Egyptian buildings, such as the pyramids. The pyramids were built as tombs for Egyptian pharaohs (kings).

You can't forget the Great Sphinx! The sphinx's head and body are carved out of one giant piece of rock! Sphinx statues were built in ancient Egypt to guard important tombs and temples.

This mosque in Timbuktu, Mali, was built from clay more than 500 years ago. Timbuktu was an important center for trade and Islamic learning from the 1300's to the 1600's.

There are also many interesting modern buildings and places in Africa. One of them is the futuristic Limete Tower in Kinshasa, the capital of the Democratic Republic of the Congo.

The Independence Arch sits in the Black Star Square in Accra, the capital of Ghana. The arch commemorates this country's independence from Great Britain in 1957.

The Mapungubwe Interpretation Centre in South Africa combines traditional building methods with the latest architectural designs to create a stunning structure.

Australia is the only place that is both a country and a continent!
I'm so special!
New Zealand and most of the Pacific Islands are part of a region called Oceania. It's home to around 22 million people!

The largest city by population in this area is Sydney, Australia. Sydney is famous for such landmarks as the Sydney Opera House and Sydney Harbour Bridge.

The Great Barrier Reef is the world's largest coral reef system. It is found off the northeast coast of Australia.

Uluru is a sacred place for the Anangu people, one of the Indigenous peoples of Australia. The rock appears to glow red at sunrise and sunset.

Bora Bora and many other islands in Oceania are popular places for tourists to visit. Tourism is important for their **economy.**

It's hard to believe, but the Moeraki Boulders in New Zealand are naturally spherical!

Aahhhhhhh! I'm bungee jumping off the Sky Tower in Auckland, New Zealand!
At 1,076 feet (328 meters) tall, it's the tallest **freestanding** structure in the Southern **Hemisphere.**

Easter Island is famous for these gigantic statues, called moai. They were carved hundreds of years ago by the Rapa Nui people, the island's first inhabitants.
That's pronounced MOH-I.

NORTH AMERICA

North America is the third largest continent by area. It is divided into 23 countries. This includes countries in Central America and those on Caribbean islands.

Around 598 million people live in North America.

Around half of them live in the United States of America (USA), the third largest country in the world by population.

Saint Kitts and Nevis is the smallest country by size and population in North America. The country is made up of two islands in the Caribbean Sea.

Mexico City is the largest city in North America by population. Around 22 million people live there—that's more than the populations of Norway, Bolivia, and Mongolia combined!

Some people mistakenly think that New York City is the capital of the United States ...

... but its capital is actually here in Washington, D.C.!
I'm in front of the Washington Monument, which was built in honor of George Washington, the first U.S. president.

There are two capital cities on the island of Hispaniola in the Caribbean Sea. The island is home to two countries: Haiti and the Dominican Republic, and their capitals—Port-au-Prince and Santo Domingo.
HAITI
DOMINICAN REPUBLIC

North America is filled with iconic buildings and structures, such as the Golden Gate Bridge in San Francisco, USA. It's one of the largest suspension bridges in the world.

Even though work began on the Crazy Horse Memorial in South Dakota, USA, in 1948, it's still not finished, due to bad weather, funding problems, and difficult construction issues!

But when it is completed, this memorial to the Native American leader Crazy Horse will be taller than the Washington Monument!

Don't look down! The CN Tower in Toronto, Canada, is the highest structure in the Western Hemisphere, measuring over 1,815 feet (553 meters) high.

Travel back in time at the ruins of Chichén Itzá, an important ancient Maya city in Mexico. The Maya were an advanced civilization that ruled over parts of Mexico and Central America before the 1500's.

Time to take a walk on the wild side through some of North America's most exciting natural places ...

... starting here at Niagara Falls on the border between the United States and Canada.
Whoahhhhh!

At Yellowstone National Park in the USA, the Grand Prismatic Spring is full of color! Its amazing hues come from tiny microbes in the water.

At Horseshoe Bend, USA, the Colorado River makes a dramatic meander, or bend.

A lake ... underground?
These large natural sinkholes in Mexico are known as cenotes. They are filled with groundwater.

SOUTH AMERICA

South America is a place with many different types of landscape and climate.

It is divided up into 12 countries and 2 dependencies.

The largest country is Brazil. It takes up about half the land and is home to about 212 million people. This is as many as all other South American countries combined!

Suriname is the smallest country by size and population. Most of the country is covered by mountainous rain forests.

Around 85 percent of people in South America live in cities and urban areas.
This colorful street is one of my favorite places in Buenos Aires, the capital city of Argentina.

São Paulo in Brazil is the most populous city in South America and the Southern Hemisphere!

La Paz, Bolivia, is the highest capital city in the world! It is located 12,500 feet (3,810 meters) above sea level in the Andes Mountains.

The capital of Brazil was moved from Rio de Janeiro to Brasília in 1960. The new city of Brasília was built in the interior of the country to encourage people to move inland.
Brasília has striking modern architecture. This is the Cathedral of Brasília!

Everyone knows that South America is home to the world's largest rain forest—the Amazon. But did you know it's also home to ...

... the world's highest waterfall?! Angel Falls in Venezuela is an amazing 3,212 feet (979 meters) tall!

... the world's largest salt flat?! The thick crust of salt that covers Salar de Uyuni in Bolivia was left behind when prehistoric lakes evaporated.
When it rains, it becomes the world's largest mirror!

... and the driest desert outside of the poles?! The Atacama Desert in Chile and Peru receives less than 0.5 inch (1.3 centimeters) of rain a year!

It's a bit of a trek up to Machu Picchu in Peru, but it's worth it! Here you can see the ruins of an Inca royal estate. The site dates from the 1400's.

You need to go even higher to appreciate the Nazca Lines! These giant designs are marked into the ground in the desert of southern Peru. They were made by the Nazca people, who lived in this area between 100 B.C. and A.D. 800.

The statue of Christ the Redeemer that overlooks Rio de Janeiro, Brazil, is one of the largest statues in the world, at 100 feet (30 meters) tall!

In the past, a land bridge connected North and South America. Thanks to the nearby Panama Canal, ships no longer have to sail all the way around South America to travel between the Atlantic and Pacific Oceans!

Speaking of engineering—the Itaipú Dam is one of the largest power plants on Earth!
It's located on the border between Brazil and Paraguay. It supplies electricity to both countries.

ANTARCTICA
Antarctica is an unusual and remarkable place. It's actually the coldest ...

... brightest ...

... and windiest continent!

No one lives permanently on Antarctica, but scientists have set up research stations where they can live and work all year round.

Antarctica isn't all ice and snow. It's also home to some exciting places, like the South Pole! This marker shows its location.

Mount Erebus is an active volcano on Ross Island, off the coast of Antarctica.

I think I'll keep my distance!

Many of the islands around Antarctica are home to colonies of penguins. They are important places because penguins breed and raise chicks there.

Where did all the snow go?

There are some places in Antarctica that aren't covered in snow. Barely any snow falls in the McMurdo Dry Valleys, and any that does fall evaporates quickly.

Hey, I'm Region!
Region and I are similar in some ways. We are both specific areas that people name to set them apart from their surroundings.

However, I'm bigger than Place. The area covered by a region also has some common features.
Let's take a look at some examples.

Have you ever heard of the Corn Belt?

No, not that kind of belt!

The Corn Belt is a region in the Midwestern United States where the climate, topography, and soil conditions are ideal for raising livestock and feed crops—especially corn.

French Canada is a region of Canada where many people speak French as their first language.
Bonjour!
Salut!

A region can be part of a larger place. For example, Siberia is the chilly northern region of Russia.

A region can also be a collection of places grouped together, such as the eleven countries that make up Southeast Asia.
SOUTHEAST ASIA

There are many different features that define a region. Let's take a look at some of them now.

PHYSICAL REGIONS

Some regions are defined by physical characteristics. This could be something as simple as location!

Sub-Saharan Africa includes all land to the south of the Sahara Desert.

A common feature of a region could be a **biome.** For example, the Pampas is a fertile grassland region that covers parts of Argentina, Brazil, and Uruguay.

A region could also be defined by its climate. Polar climate regions are found around the north and south poles. The weather there is very cold all year round!

Regions can be defined by the natural resources found there ...
The Appalachian Mountains in the USA is a coal-mining region.

... or by topography (the height and shape of land features in an area) ...
Monument Valley is a desert region of the states of Utah and Arizona, USA, known for its many massive sandstone buttes.

... or even its type of soil!
Regions with many active volcanoes often have fertile soil. Volcanic ash makes the soil particularly rich in nutrients—even if the eruptions happened years ago!

Some regions of natural beauty are given special names to make them stand out as tourist destinations. The Lake District is a region in the north of Britain with many ... you guessed it ... lakes!

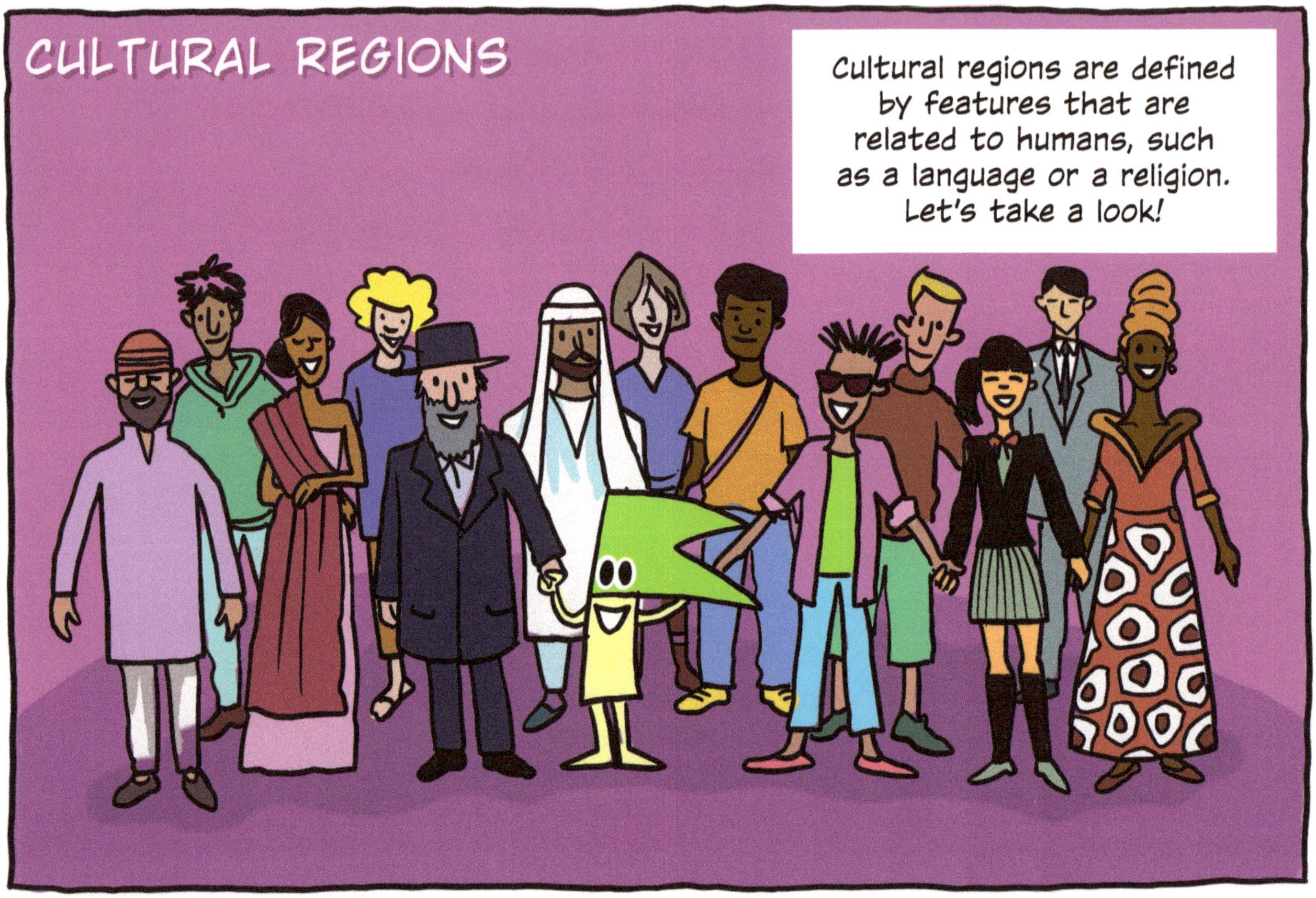

CULTURAL REGIONS

Cultural regions are defined by features that are related to humans, such as a language or a religion. Let's take a look!

Latin America is a region in North and South America where people mainly speak languages that are derived from Latin, such as Spanish, Portuguese and French. This region includes all of the land south of the United States of America.

In some regions, many people follow the same religion. For example, Islam is a widely practiced religion in the South Asia and Southeast Asia regions.

Regions are also born from a common history.

Celtic regions include Ireland, and parts of the United Kingdom and France. Here, the ancient culture of the Celts was preserved. Today, these regions share similar Celtic languages and traditions.

Regions can also be defined by their economy. Developed regions have more complex economies than developing regions. The level of development can affect the income and quality of life of the people who live there.

Cultural regions don't have clear borders. They often overlap physical boundaries or national borders. People may disagree on the boundaries of a particular cultural region.

The region where they live is often an important part of a person's identity. People enjoy celebrating their regional customs and traditions, such as food, music, and dance.

POLITICAL REGIONS

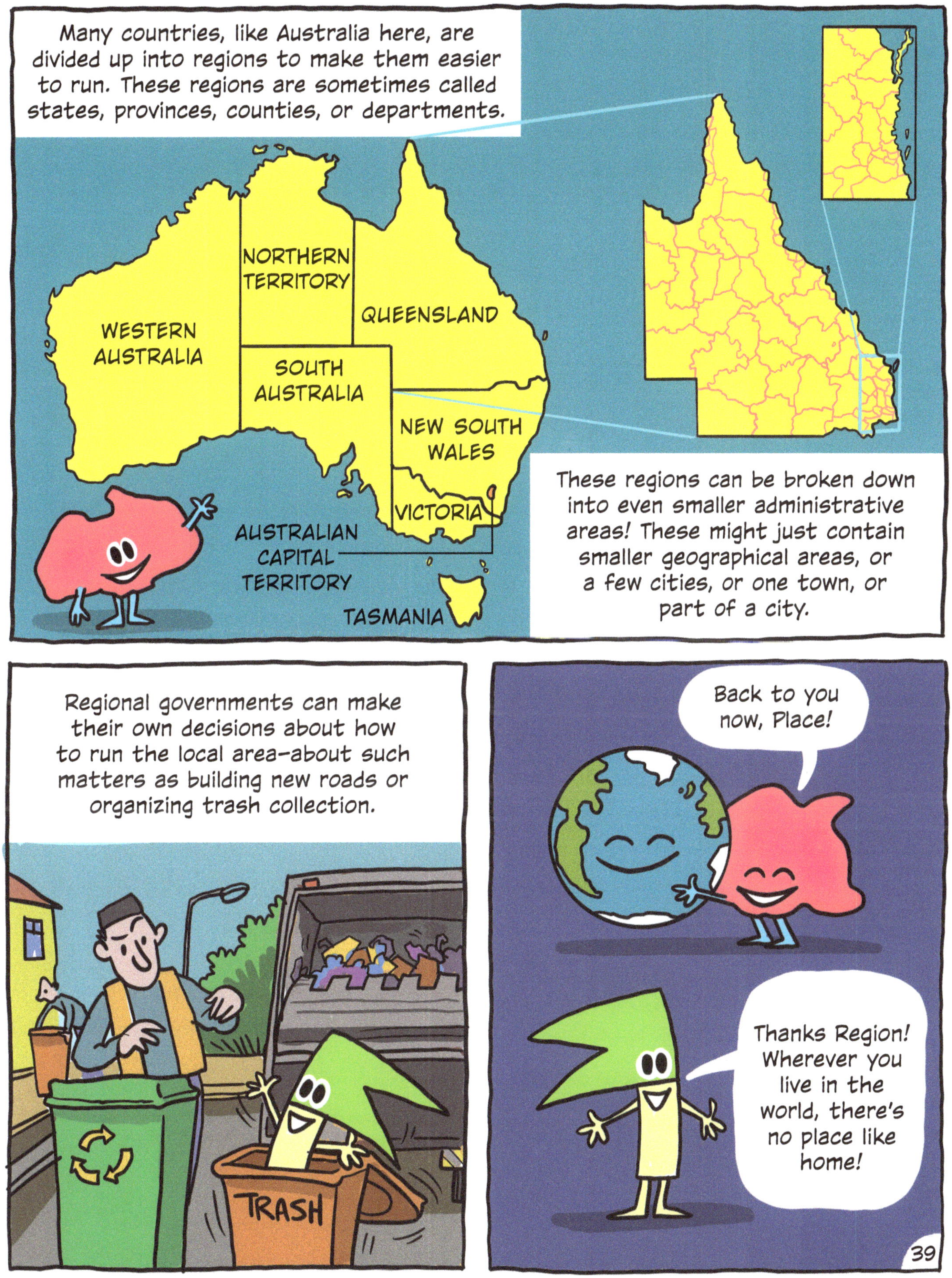

Regional governments can make their own decisions about how to run the local area—about such matters as building new roads or organizing trash collection.

WORDS TO KNOW

biome a specific environment that is home to living things suited for that place and climate.

civilization the culture or way of life in a society or country at a particular time.

dependency a country that is supported and governed by another country.

economy how a country makes and spends money.

fertile describes soil in which plants grow well.

freestanding standing alone without any supports.

futuristic very modern, as if from the future.

hemisphere one of the Earth's two halves.

independent freedom from being ruled by another country.

Indigenous the first people who lived in an area before all others.

landlocked having no coast and surrounded by the land of other countries.

landmark a building or place that is easily recognized and is representative of a particular place.

mainland the main part of a country or continent and not including any islands around it.

monument a building or structure built to honor something or someone special.

mountain range a group or line of mountains.

population all of the people living in a particular area.

populous describes an area with lots of people living in it.

prehistoric before written records.

rural relating to the countryside.

topography the arrangement of physical features in an area.

union a political group of several regions.

urban relating to towns or cities.